LONE

POETRY IN A YEAR
OF LOCKDOWN

JASMINE CHE

JASMINE CHE

ACCOMPANYING AUDIO

Hello poetry lover!

Thank you for making a purchase to help and support the life of this book.
As an extra thanks, I have narrated an audio book that you can access freely to enhance your experience whilst reading.

Please visit:
tinyurl.com/LonePoetryAudio

I'd love to hear how you've found the book! It really makes my day when I hear from readers! Please let me know through your review on Amazon or Goodreads. You can email me at jasminewrites@outlook.com or send a hello to my IG found at the end!

Big love to you,

Jasmine

LONE

DEDICATED TO

Every person who endured the Covid lockdowns, suffered, struggled, laughed, played, and are stronger now because of it.

(That's you).

And to those we have lost during this time.

"POETRY OF THE HEART
COMPELS THE HAND"

CONTENTS

I'd like to mention that these poems are a selection written and compiled during an extended Covid lockdown that I undertook from January 2020 to June 2021*.
A longer period of time than most to endure, yet, has proved to be a hermitual time for deep reflection, renewal and transformation.

Creating LONE has been a rich process, to more clearly see the slivers of silver, what I have learnt and obstacles overcome. Hence, the poems are not sequenced in chronological order, rather are in such a way to make sense of this rollercoaster journey. I imagine this will make for a more pleasant reading experience for you, as you dip into facets of my lockdown.

The emotions present are very varied and subject matter too. I've used poetry as a means to express that which I feel in the very moment, to the best of my ability. If you read and are concerned for my mental health, fret not.
I am only displaying a spectrum of emotions that we as humans so colourfully can embody. Rather, poetry and writing has been a cathartic means of release, a way to process situations or to explore imagined avenues.

*I was shielding to protect my sister, Bunny, whom is in the extremely vulnerable group. To mention, there were occasions I would be able to be free for outings, though these were scattered and infrequent. Roughly, 8 months with Bunny alone, the rest with family still shielding.

How funny it is – I had been longing for a meditation retreat for a while, prior to the emergence of Covid. Some things are strange, when we get what we ask for. To be honest, I really enjoyed the first few months, and was thankful to not be missing out as the world had stopped too. Then, the retreating turned serious.

If anyone has been on an intensive meditation retreat, you'll know it isn't *really* about wellness, feeling your omms, and having a chill. But, actually is a mentally, emotionally and physically intense test of endurance – **all the time**. Things always hits the fan, and you're left there to juggle it all: thoughts, feelings, work, problems, trauma and people, with little room for escape.
So, congratulations on your **first** and **second** retreat!

As a seasoned retreater and meditator, I've found what carries one through is what we do for our self, at every level. For me, it was the breathing exercises to climb back into the eye of the storm – the present, writing to give the mind some space, eating well – my aim was for restaurant quality, consistent meditation, trying to maintain sleeping routines, focusing on my goals and desires I could achieve, movement, video calls with others, and a lot, a lot of self care.

Now, for poetry!

OPEN-ENDED JOURNEYS

One must acknowledge
That being lone
Does not necessitate
Feeling alone.

That being supported
Does not pre-dictate
Rich transformation.

It has been a gift
To have precious few
Surround me in form,
Unmistakably close.

While others although
physically estranged,
Troop through the
ether.

During this lone period,
I am given apt context
In which to find myself.

It is difficult to love a grey cladded day,

I look for the hues of blue

in the cotton buds of the sky.

The transition from a rich crescent dark

that makes twinkles of every early riser

to a transient greying.

No peep of Sun that laughs,

just the scrambling of a soul

trying to find comfort in this world.

In the quiet of these moments,

My mind is full of litany,

Tongue gripped in silence,

Arms at the ready, twitching.

An upswelling in my chest,

Anguish flaming the lip of my silence

As the water fills my cup,

Mind frantically seeks to bequeath

A world with scores of song.

Yet, I am rusty,

My pen in hand

Forgets the..

Has a..

Y2000 connection to my soul.

JASMINE CHE

- Let me be brave, especially at a time of such opportunity where many others too are reworking, resetting their lives.

- Let me do things without needing a particular reason to do so, other than wanting to.

- Let me rise to challenges with the confidence and boldness I possess.

- Let me pursue ideas that I enjoy, even if they have no fruit in sight/in mind.

- Let me stand tall and emboldened by expression.

- Let me be who I am, with flaws and all.

- Let me just show up to life with whatever I have and possess.

- Let me reach out to people in my periphery who might love to hear from me.

- Let me write to friends and loved ones, sending an article, trinket or gift to let them know they were in my thoughts.

Lockdown brings threads of the past back into light.

Sweet achings of desired release.

Finding closure in flowerbeds we thought lay dead,

barren and forgotten,

only to rise with bewitching power of cyclical hunger.

Forget-me-nots, remember-me-if-you-wills,

bursting upwards,

bringing forth bells-blue that entrance

back and forth in winds harsh,

Filament clappers singing ancient songs

of quiet misery.

Dare I tread?

Watch

how

you

step.

Fixations upon fixations.
Are we mistaken?
We miss beauty parading seasons
with mind-wandering...
Only the icy-tongued kisses

Rosening cheeks and
shallowing breath we feel.
Gentle reminders to
Luxuriate in heat meets frost,
Notice boundaries and open.

Trust in preparation,
Step firm in fields unknown.
Seek resolve in foreign journeys
for we have grown
with every minute of every day.

Claim your confidence.
Opponents are only armed with
fetters of the mind.
Befriend oneself, trust ones nature.
Such are boundaries worth crossing.

I notice how emotional I am.
I notice how my heart swells,
Feels full,
Yet at times so empty.

I see my heart race in an instance,
Body waving with tension.

In this current moment,
I am so full in love with my partner,
Appreciative of all in my life.

I notice how my moods are volatile.
How so willing I am to be swept
Into gales of emotion.

I fall into highs,
See lows that nip at my toes.

In a moment, my feet can be
Knocked off
unsteady...

I feel like a child that falls,

Falls again,

But sees all the joys,
Getting back up to play.

-

I find it important to steady
My breath,
Present, with what is.

At times I am willing
To fall into it all.
Give everything up to a whim,
To be carried
By aimless
Raging emotion alone.

It is powerful.
It is intoxicating.
It is life in free reign.

PLANT JOURNEYS

Live with

presence

+

gratitude shall

come naturally

We wrote a poem

The tree and I,

Together we stood,

It held my cry.

Rooting me deep,

Into the Earth,

So I had space,

To be well heard.

A little while

It listened to me

The gentle soul

Set my mind free.

I raised my chin,

To the true sky,

The kerfuffle you see,

Had passed me by.

A single tear

Rolled from my eye.

Now I could see,

What was true,

That life beats,

Wind blows,

For us

To dance

- To flow.

THE TREE TOLD ME

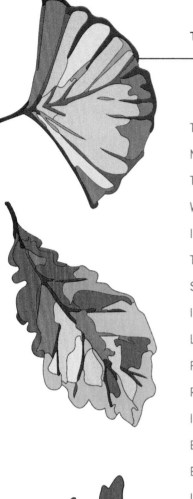

The tree told me
Not to be afraid
To ground myself,
Work on my foundations.
It beckoned me
To see its fallen
Spreadeagled leaves;
It's memories
Laid down in glory
For all to see.
Revel in its riches.
It told me
Each was special,
Enjoyed,
Loved fully.

Love fully,
Regret not.
The passing of time
Is the silver,
Binding stories.

JASMINE CHE

Cry not,
Fret not,
Far from lossless
It knew that soon
It would be leafless,
But has treasured
fully, its life.

That to hibernate
Was a time of rest.

To again
Rebloom,
Reawaken,
To be reborn,
Carrying the wisdom
of sages and cycles
once more.

The tree told me:

Dance with the wind

Spread your roots

Lay your foundations

Feel sun on your face

Worries appear fierce

But the subtleties

Of life's joys,

Sensations in full

Have worries falter,

Step back,

Join hands to waltz

As they always were.

Today, I am repotting myself.

Giving some more room to breathe,

To be me,

To be free from my incessant

Mind

Thinkings.

Where I have outgrown my environment,

Learned,

Absorbed what I needed.

I am better;

Vibrant,

Flourishing.

Acclimatising to change

May take some getting used to,

But it will give me all I need to be.

[Physical repot 4x in the past 6 months]

[7 times in 12 months]

What a wild journey.

UNEASY JOURNEYS

I love the honesty of our eyes
They never, never, never lie.
Bewitched you may be
With what you see in the mirror
But that smile, can't hide,
The sadness tickling your eye.

They never, never, never lie.

My sister told me of your eyes,
She saw loneliness that lurked,
A quiet melancholy creeped,
"Be careful," she said,
"You'll be collateral".

They never, never, never lie.

Actions were shown,
Gestures wonderful and played
On the strings of my heart,
I was yours to keep,
For as long as
You'd have me.

But those eyes

They never, never, never lie.

Mine were bright, twinkly,
But what I saw in the mirror,
Could never save me,
As starlight would fade,
The closer we seek, we go,
We reach glowing, flickering coal.

My eyes,

They never, never, never lie.

You were never mine to keep,
But I was always yours,
Funny the way it is,
I can't even change a thing,
Because, your eyes they know,
That you are always yours,
Yours alone.

Your eyes,

They never, never, never lie.

Mine cry,

Oh how they cry.

Would I leave you,

Love you more,

If our eyes were

Adorned with the dew of dawn?

Would it be sweet

If we met unannounced

By cocktail magick'd spells

whispering enclosed fury?

Or will it be

That our hands might sleep

Inches away each morning

With eyes wide,

Fixated on left to rights

Harnessed in shadows overnight

Aching for mooring?

Where do I go if you
Are the first place I turn to,
When I am lost,
in need,
stuck..

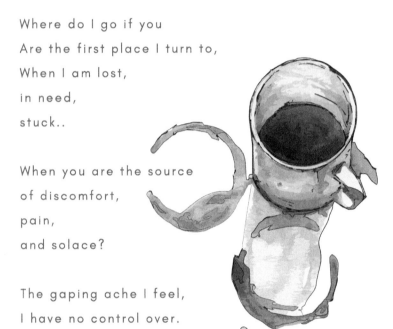

When you are the source
of discomfort,
pain,
and solace?

The gaping ache I feel,
I have no control over.

There is only but to sit,
Feel.
Brace.
Temper the undulating waves
of frustration
jostling from within.

WHAT AM I TO YOU?

I don't want to see you
for an hour,
then have you leave,
without a care..
Like I am some checklist
to be seen,
ticked,
left,
in glory or accomplished.

To watch you,
See,
Hug,
Revel,
Delight,
In a past lover's embrace.

You leave.
I am discarded;
A tissue,
delicate,
useful
at the time,
but left to feel
like for that moment,
I would just be that:

Serving a purpose
- nothing more.

My body errs on sensations
Of a past breakup.
Frustrative losslessness invading,
Pulsations nothing quite qualms,
Except writing plentiful textos to you.

Key melodies vibrate away,
In brushing letters with furiocity.
Feels of hopelessness arise,
As if we are ending...
That we **must** end.

Although, I cannot be sure if it is
My neural networks firing
{patterns ending things with X2],
Or if it is actually me,
and my compatibility with you...

Mismatched in centrifugal, isolating risings.

*

Will we sync up?

I stand unsure

Do I love you?

Yes, I concur –

This is the reason

Why we got this far.

To me, you are my North Star.

But did I read the book,

You bought on constellations?

No.

Am I an avid astrologer?

Perhaps so.

Is this all ego illusion?

I do not know,

But its trying me.

I feel like a mad lady In my thoughts,

Writing this so you know of sorts.

I'm doing my very best...

As these raging hormones contest

What is at the heart of the matter.

INDULGE ME

And I am wanting,

That you'll stop dead-in-your-tracks,

After reading my poetry,

Living up to my idealistic illusions,

That you'll blow off

Whatever was scheduled,

To run back home,

Knock on the door

And caress me.

Hold me,

In your safety,

But I know,

You won't.

What if:

It turns out to be

That I am not as committed as

I thought I was...

That my clutching,

In holding on so tight,

Is a reflection of my insecure

Foundations,

Dating,

back,

To when I was young?

What if it is:

That I am not

As committed as I said

I was going to be?

That I might break your heart

Because of the story,

I saw unfold when I was young,

Which made me think

That true love endings was for others,

But,

Not for me.

Its not that I expect things to last forever,

Its just that I thought we'd last a little longer.

I don't blame you.

I don't blame me either.

Sometimes its the context in which we live.

We always do our best, I believe.

No ill harm,

No hatred,

Disguised confusion.

Some things are just out of our control.

We can only try to navigate.

Release any expectation.

Carry hope.

Continuing to do our best,

Be honest,

Be vulnerable,

Be true to ourselves,

Share wildly.

MY DEAR LOVE

My dear love,

It is Spring,

Just as beautiful as the last,

Cherry blossoms burst forth,

Showering those walking below

In a fragrant haze,

Intoxicated - I stumble.

I see you amongst those

Queuing for coffee.

I hear your laughter

In the warm wind.

It was this time last year

Where our walks were freer.

I glance over,

Stumbling, the bench catches me,

Ragged my breath

Calls for you.

You reach out to hold my hand.

I can't feel it. But I know.

Surrendering, I soften,

Close my eyes.

I see you, clear as day.

I am okay.

I am okay.

We are okay.

TENDER JOURNEYS

Take me bare, as I am,

Not how you want me,

To be,

Take me freely.

Caress me,

Tease me,

Graze your hand against mine

In your arms, hold me divine.

Like you have nothing to hide.

We will watch the world

From between inky silken sheets

As we coalesce,

Heartbeats.

X

_____

We could slide...
Sticky sweet saliva
dripping chocolate.

Heaving breath
reveals standing hairs
on the curve of my back.

Our lips collide,
fingers grazing
soft supple skin.

Gently,
your hands find
contours of my face,
tracing them delicately.

I fall further:
supported, embraced
in warm arms, enveloping
folds of fabric amidst
golden fairy light.

Eyes widen to meet
mischievous coy smiles.

WHIRLING JOURNEYS

It is in the space
we fall
which is essential.
When we are alone,
we remember
our brilliance.

In our slumps,
And the pit,
The decision comes
To fall in the
never-ending abyss,
Or to fly.

Tonight, I was on the brink
of spiralling out of control.
Responsibility held me so tight,
I wanted to write a message of fleeing.

Erase myself off the face of the Earth:
Off the radar, contacting no one,
Living my life undetected,
aloof and emotionally unavailable.

I realise:

I will probably, likely, never be

as beautiful as I am in this instance,

I will not have the same vitality

coursing through my veins.

So why do the carrara walls

guarding my thrumming heart,

quake as I watch glimmers of newness?

My mind:

wild, snarling, untamed,

threatening offence

as I simply sit, open and lay,

Lay down the worries and fears

I thought I'd befriended...

Yet still, I wrestle with my mind

With all its imaginings.

RAIN, FEELS, MICE

Sometimes it feels too much,

not psychologically,

but the intensity of feeling is so strong.

Powerful waves crescendo within.

My fragile confines

simply cannot contain it.

So I release the seeping rivulets.

I command the rain to stop.

One simply cannot handle another storm

It rattles the boundaries,

Threatens to split apart the house

with crashes of lighting.

So with petrified mice

I hide away.

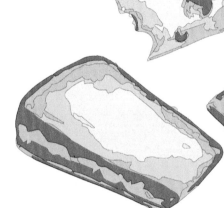

But rain can cleanse,

leave things afresh.

To what extent the magnitude

It can leave mudslides..

Ruin lives..

No two storms are the same.

How well is the home built?

Of stone?

Of cheese?

Trembling in the slightest hints of thunder?

I will only know,

When I let it rain.

I rage
Against convention.
A barricaded wall
Surmounts my tender body
- I clutch my drawn cards.

Whether I win,
Depends on the game
We play.

Dealer says:
"Your choice, same cards."

In a game of lottery,
We experience loss,
But not defeat.

Yet the games I play,
I compete against all,
And lose against myself.

Tranquil on the river
Out toward the sea.
Didn't notice the edge
Was coming for me.

I was comfortable,
In a blurry haze,
This struggle I do know;
Anicha is the call.

Yet the mind only dreams
That it is not   – blink –
When it all becomes real,
Right on the very brink.

Everything heightened
The moment one sights
Enemy, gaze tightens
Preparing to fight...

Down the waterfall,

I

fall

.

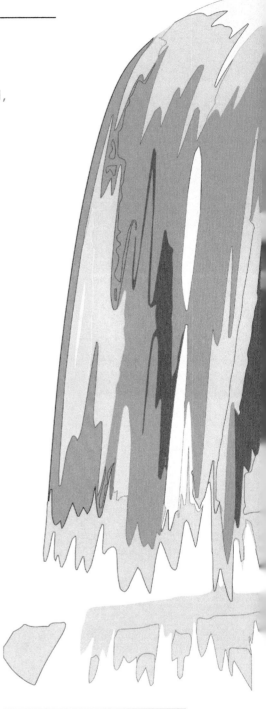

JASMINE CHE

"**Help!**" I sound.

-

But all there is,

Is masked

By the beatdown.

I want to cry,

I want to sleep,

I want to scroll,

get away from the heap...

Nestling inside.

Can't I watch it as I scroll?

The feelings lessen,

It becomes tolerable.

Its a baby that cries,

I, the exhausted mum verges

On crying with them.

"Hellloooooooooooooooooooooooooooooo,"

it screams,

Like it's shouting at the mountain top.

"HUSH! Be quiet!" I cry.

"An avalanche will awaken and then,

we'll all be pretty fucked."

"The avalanche is good!" it screams louder.

"It's natural!

A flood of solid water cascading...

It's nature just doing its thing."

Here I am,

clutching myself,

my knees.

"Please, please make the rumbling stop!"

"This avalanche will happen.

Whether its now or later,

Just remember,

Later, there will be more snow."

A dull silence enters...

I am back to not sleeping, not eating.

Trick me not,

Is it lunchtime already?

I cannot bear another slice of bread;

A candida prison of carbs.

Lockdown woes of continuous rattling,

Of pots,

Stirring,

Pans strewn.

EAT, COOK, CLEAN, REPEAT.

A mantra of: physicality-brought woe.

It must be: first world problems indeed,

But how: is one to work on one's dreams?

EAT,

     COOK,

         CLEAN,

            REPEAT.

I could lie and say I like it like this,
But I don't.

There is a silver lining,
Boundless on one end,
Restrictive on the other side.
Joy can arise,
Otherwise: coupled tension,
The need to fulfil.

I tread on this fine line,
At times on the edge,
Paralysed; indecision.

I don't need more information,
Only an intensity of awareness
That permits time to slow,
Be motionless
And know
The steps
And where to go.

Heavy minutes seep into my skin,

    These legs trudge so begrudgingly.

Fog.   T h i c k.   *Billows* in my mind.

  Awake I blink,

    But it feels not so.

  Awake I dream

    To surges of energy met before.

  On my knees I pray:

    Let gratitude be my song.

  With each breath I beg

    To be anchored in present vitality.

HEALING JOURNEYS

If nothing else,

let me nurture my

Garden of Che.

"You often feel tired, not because you've done too much, but because you've done too little of what excites you, makes you feel alive and sparks a light in you."
SIMON ALEXANDER ONG

When I was a child, perhaps five or six, I would wear shoes that were too small. I didn't complain about the pain as I didn't want to be a nuisance to my parents who were out, working all day – so I didn't ask for new shoes.

Such a habit mentally stuck with me through the years. Over time, it wasn't shoes that I put on that didn't fit, but equally unfitting: the mentalities and personal ethea of others. In an effort to make my family proud and not cause them reason to be concerned, I fulfilled the daughter and sibling role I believed they wished.

Consistently, I found myself swayed by others. I would make decisions that led me to chase rainbows half-heartedly, or find my way to the pot of gold, only to find myself feeling no more validated than before. For some time, I was markedly unfulfilled, burnt out and rather confused. Indeed, I was on a wild-goose chase to find my happiness, using a compass governed by others.

Where was my joy?
What was the meaning to live if what we
pursued did not even bring happiness?
What would make me happy?

These questions come to me time and time again. When contemplating such questions I try practice self-kindness:

give myself ample time and space, and the means to express and explore freely, even if those around me could not/do not understand.

I shall always continue to give myself the permission and freedom to exercise choice, so I may find even greater contentment and happiness. Holding myself in this manner and making new decisions has allowed me to feel more whole, true to who I am and is my way of learning from the years before; exploring knowledge through action.

Choosing differently isn't easy, but we can learn and get better at it with every decision we make.

Here are some avenues to explore:

- **Finding what excites you**, brings you joy is one way in.

- **Noticing you are tired** of the current phase in your life is another. What changes **need** to be made?

- **What does your body say?**
  Listen to yourself, because we are always being guided to greater awareness - you already know inside what's best for you, even if you can't see or understand it.

If in this moment you can only hear the voices of others, then frequently pause and take time in silence to better hear your own sweet voice and the voice of your body.

In time, it shall reveal itself to you. This in itself, will give you the best shoes you may ever walk with in your life.
I try my best to wear these everyday.

If during this lockdown, you have struggled...

Just know you have not been alone.

I will sit by you and vouch that it has been

tremendously trying at times.

Coming out after this lockdown,

just because it may be getting back

to what feels normal...

It doesn't mean you need to be okay right away.

Keep seeking help from those around you,

You do not need the pandemic as a reason.

You always are worthy of love.

Take your time to heal.

What would your younger self think

about you as you are now?

About the work you do daily

and the life you lead?

Would they be proud

of who you are?

(be kind to yourself in answering

these - if its helpful, answer from

the perspective of a loving friend)

I have a friend here,

Who warms my soul,

Uplifts me and leaves me enthralled,

With her love,

Her passion and gentle fire,

That wisps my hair covering my face,

Tucking them behind my ear.

We may not always see eye to eye,

But I know she holds me dear.

Jasmine, **I am proud of...**
Jasmine, **I forgive myself for...**
Jasmine, **I am thankful for...**
Jasmine, **I allow myself to...**

This exercise is said aloud in front of a mirror, looking at oneself directly in the eye, or, written down. It is used to give ourselves the space to verbalise, acknowledge ourselves, be appreciated, be loved, to be.

The more often you do this exercise, the richer it becomes and the more emotion you will feel during the practice. If any strong emotions or sensations occur, keep repeating the phrase until it clears the heart space and isn't painful or uncomfortable anymore. We are allowing ourselves to integrate these emotions through gentle acceptance.

Often these may be phrases we may not have been told when we were younger but needed to hear. With this practice, we gift these words to ourselves.

Replace your name where you see mine - "Jasmine".

When I am in pain (physical or emotional) I ask: what is the **nicest, most supportive** thing I can do for myself right now?

Hold space if I need: to cry, hug myself, reassure myself, allow myself to release, meditate, reach out to friends, journal and acknowledge the pain.

I'll think to **nourish myself**: warm the body, self massage, drink tea, listen to soothing music, sleep early, take a bath, rest, chill out.

Make me a priority.

Joining others this lockdown, I re-assessed my needs.
Finding that I wanted to be in a *better* relationship with
myself.

Here's my (aspirational, non-exhaustive) checklist:

- [ ] Wear glitter, sleep more + allow myself intentional rest.
- [ ] Pay myself some respect daily.
- [ ] Take myself on dates: cute, frivolous, well-planned.
- [ ] Early 5AM mornings because I think that's boss.
- [ ] Be the best work partner for myself.
- [ ] Take small actions in line with the me
   I'll always admire & who I aspire to be.
- [ ] Return daily to rest in this heart-home of mine.
- [ ] Feel ease and alive in my body, mind, spirit.
- [ ] Do things on my bucket list unapologetically,
   (writing this poetry book is one of them)
- [ ] Have fun, show off & flirt with myself.
- [ ] Treat myself if that's what I want.
- [ ] Buy ourself our dream house.
- [ ] Find happy in my dress.
- [ ] Stay true to my word.

And for you?

TO CALM A WORRIED YOU

Here is my ultimate lockdown toolkit of self-management techniques. Even in my most breathless and challenging of moments, a combination of these found me peaceful refuge. The more practised you are, the easier it will be.

- Connect with the **breath**
  - 6 deep breaths kicks in our regulatory system, but the more the better

- Re-inhabit the **body**
  - Do a scan of each body part, massage the area with your hands to bring back lost sensation / relieve pain or tension if present
  - What does the body tell you it needs to feel better?

- **Guard** your mind from harmful mental images and thoughts
  - Think not too much of far-fetched calamities - be aware of your mind telling you these stories, know they are not currently real, only **imagined**
  - Tell your mind that they not helpful. Like a cat bringing back dead birds... Thank it, then discard and ask it bring back more useful thoughts

JASMINE CHE

- **Write** every last: anxiety causing/ illogical/ nonsensical/ very real worries   down, so they have a space to live (**outside** your precious brain)
    - On the list, what can you control? Put a ring around them
    - Write an immediate action you can take to positively influence or bring back control for each
    - For everything else remind yourself: you can't control things you can't control, so you will sure do your best to make a difference to things you can

- **Affirm and remind** yourself:
    - Your best is enough.
        - "I do my best, I forget the rest."
    - Trust in who you are, which has already taken you this far.
        - "I trust myself, I trust the process, I trust in my abilities to make a difference."
    - Heart-centred actions are pure, straightforward and devoid of any mental or intellectual convolutions. When you get there, you'll know what the next step is.
        - "One step, one action at a time."
    - Write/ say aloud all your qualities and resources that will help you.

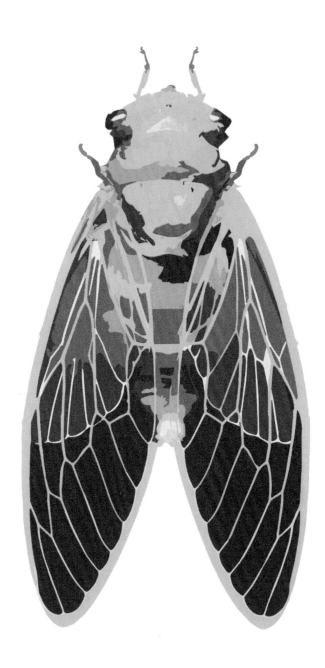

POEM OF THE EVENING

As I sit,

Awakened in thought,

A chrysalis appears,

Twinkling green of cicadas,

A dish,

Unbeknownst to me,

Calling me.

I do not have fear

But rather

Awakened,

I dream -

Of felonies of good,

Where light does not exist

Without the shadow casted

Reflections of the light,

Mirrored in our eyes.

What the future holds,

I know not,

But I hold;

Release:

My breath in anticipation,

Awaiting to delight

In the joys of this world.

MODERN DAY LADY

Contingencies hold me
In circumstantial parallels.
A lady of leisure
Taken by modern silk roads.
Simple observation,
Pressing of buttons
Has allowed
freedoms

unparalled;

Giving the means,
For this heart to write.

JASMINE CHE

Attention
energises,
Intention
transforms

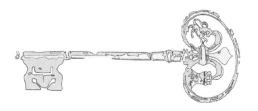

FREE FLY

I write until the fire is quenched.
The niggling releases its grip
On my will,
Our will.

I speak free.

Unrestrained by all before me;
Those who wish to shackle,
Dancing flames alight in crackle,
Quietening these forced hands.

No one can silence winds
That blow through evergreens
Of my luscious forest.

Leave me wild,
As the day I was born.

Kiss me,
Free - as a bird.

A NOVEMBER DAY IN BRIGHTON

Beach walking,

The tousled ground beneath freerunners

Promises for another day

To come back bare.

Sun-kissing delight,

Undressing, part hidden

In the comfort of soft palazzos.

Piers at vertical with the sea

Inching to 270.

Yearning to be set ablaze,

A return to health,

I fear it not too late,

On this beach of solitude.

LET GO

At the edge of letting go,
Red embers flicker from my body,
Ravenous and searching.
Eager to let loose - emotion,
Stir   -   rile things up,
Catch on kindling unaware.

"*Danger*!" A voice cautions,
"Careful what you set alight
For it is all in the ego,
What is wrong and who's right?"

Embers blaze a little stronger,
I realise.. I'd be burning
Internal, precious..

With a deep breath,
Channelling fire deep within:

"Emerge, find solace, be set free."

Ahhhhhhh...

Heartsong,
Was it you I was looking for?
The never-ending door
key I've been crying for?

Years silent,
Trapped,
Ignored,
I didn't know how to..

I'd find you
But walk away,
Never realising
To stay..

Made the sighing:
Deeper,
Full,
Warm.

Replacing the aching
Lull of quiet anguish -
Beckoning to come see,
Listen and free,

But I didn't know how.

ONE - OPEN

Hand on my chest
I'd sit,   I'd wait.
Sometimes I'd walk
When hearing the call.

Only to feel
Grief pull at ones feet.
Semblances of joy.
U n e a s e.

Sometimes my eyes ran
Leagues of slivers
Glistening gold
Against my cheek.

-

Alas,   I hear it!
Scribble down the code,
Unlocked it again.
Surely, this time I'll remember...

I'll pay a visit daily
Bringing sunflowers
To reflect that
Which warms within.

With each day
Lonely not will I be
I'm not afraid *anymore*
You see.

TO MY PAST AND FUTURE

I hope that if I have a child,
She will feel loved as herself.
That she does not need a man.
To learn this from the way I am.

I hope she looks at herself with love,
With intense, unwavering pride.
That she sees beauty and wonder
She wells naturally abundantly inside.

I hope she knows that every day
She is truly blessed.
That she has support and nourishment
To find fulfilment and her best.

I hope she will fulfil her dreams,
Be a force of good.
I hope she is kind and takes the time
To make everyone understood.

I hope she feels loved
Just as she is.
I hope she treasures moments in bliss,
With nothing amiss.

This is too, what I want for me.
I hope young Jasmine gets to see.
I hope she can be set free,
Through this vicarious opportunity.

I

am

this one

singular drop

.

A complexity of

parts Distilled into one

passionately writhing drop

.

Where you can taste the sea,

the trees, sounds of my ukelele

.

I gleam, As I hold inside – My

Garden of Che, As it blooms

and thrives

.

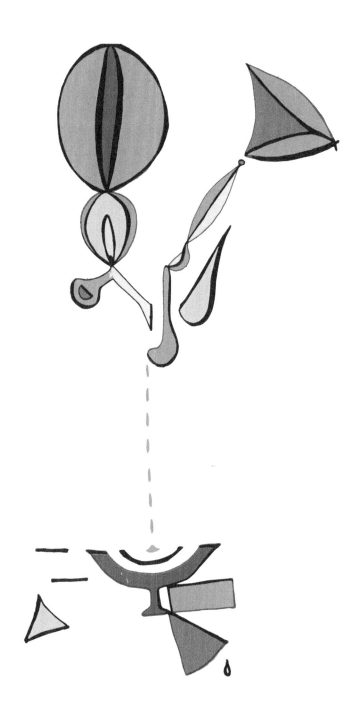

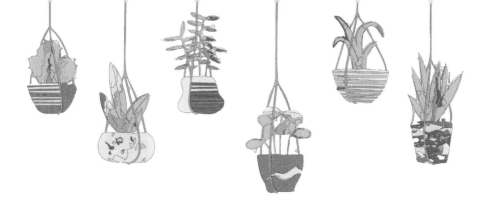

ABOUT THE AUTHOR

Jasmine Che is a poet and artist who lives in Blackheath, London.

She has a longstanding practice of meditation and mindfulness and helps share mindfulness and emotional intelligence with others as an ambassador of the Federal Association of Emotional Intelligence and a certified Search Inside Yourself Leadership Institute teacher.

This feeds into her writings, recordings, and as co-host of the Awake In meditation podcast.

Jasmine shares a flat with her younger sister, 117 needy houseplants and can be found starting new projects or businesses or engaged in cooking experiments.

WHERE TO CONNECT

Ways to Connect with Jasmine Che

Instagram
@thelifeofjasmineche – personal, art, poetry nights
@thegardenofche –plant care, cooking, lifestyle

LinkedIn *– jasmineche-eiexpert*

Mindfulness - facilitator – individuals and corps
Mindful Visionaries
www.mindfulvisionaries.com

Meditation - teacher – free and live teachings
via Insight Timer App
Teacher profile: *Jasmine Che*

Awake-In Podcast – host – discussing meditation
www.awake-in.com
Listen on Youtube and Spotify

Emotional Intelligence – **ambassador** – education
The Federal Association of Emotional Intelligence
www.faei.eu

SPECIAL THANKS

To Declan for being a safe refuge to share my thoughts and work, holding space for my wildly strong emotions, and his loving words.

To my Dad who I feel somehow has genetically passed down his poetic abilities - I say genetically because I can't understand his Vietnamese poems and nor him mine - so it must be in the blood.

To my Mum for my first journal when I was 6 and for strongly advocating writing - which alighted my affinity with the pen.

To Vu, Khanh, Mimi and Cindy for your support in tangible and intangible ways.

To Avena for such warmth, nurture, and empowering conversations - pivotal in deciding to becoming an artist.

To Patrick for endless conversations on all things emotions, the icky and delicious, being such a rock for me and sharing your wisdom.

To Mr Grant, Mrs Berrill, Mr Dave, Ms Gillingham for your tutelage in Art and Writing.

To Nat, James, Antonio, Ocean, Lisa, Bill, Carolina, Isis, Mihnea, Karina, Duc, Aurora for supporting my creative pursuits, being such good friends and positive influences during this time.

To Nic, Claire FY, Sol, Leona for being true fans.

To all those who support the book with their light energy and feedback: Esti, Cristiane, Julie-Yara, Loen, Marcus, Shamash, Kwame, Steve James, Claire C, James K, Phil, Keith, Xavier, Timalka, Casandra, Viviane.

To the creatives who have inspired some of my drawings or renders of specified works: Doris Whisker - Avalanche - Avalanche, Vivian Mineker, Petra Braun - Wild Card - Slumber, Sculpd - Don't fret, Zipcy - Take me bare, Georgianna Lane, Caterina3dfeel - Seasons, The Light Seer's Tarot Fool Card, Fyodor Pavlov's Fool Card, Yoshi Yotani's Fool Card, ehoriginal - Silk Road.

To Bao-An for being patient with me, when she'd rather we dance.

ACCOMPANYING AUDIO

Hello again!

To enhance your experience,
listen to your the audio
version of LONE!

Here is the link for unlimited access:

tinyurl.com/LonePoetryAudio

Thank you so much for supporting the book
and my creative expression!

P.S. You may enjoy other audio pieces of
mine that you can find on the Insight Timer
app, where I guide you through calming
meditations, as well as other poetry
readings shared on my instagram or my
Awake-In.com podcast.

HOW DID YOU FIND IT?

This was my first book! A long-time waiting to be checked off on my bucket-list!

I'd love to hear your experience when reading LONE, as I never know how it lands. Honestly, it makes my day when I hear from readers. Let me know your thoughts through a review on Amazon or Goodreads.

Alternatively, you can send a hello to my IG or email me any questions and feedback to jasminewrites@outlook.com!

Also, if you'd like to buy a physical signed copy, use or share my book, please enquire via email.

Yours,

Jasmine

Printed in Great Britain
by Amazon

65431557R10058